~ CJ Moore's Ba

Bachelorette Classified Dating Guide

Do you keep meeting Mr. Wrong? Are you searching for the perfect man of your dreams only to come up empty? Many women are looking for love in all the wrong places! Sometimes we are so focused on finding "a man" that we are blind to what we really want in a man so we attract Mr. Wrong! By using the Law of Attraction in the *correct manner,* you can manifest and attract the ultimate man!

~ CJ Moore's Bachelorette Classified Dating Guide ~

Contents

How the law of attraction works	3
Relationship review	7
Relationship red flags	8
Self-esteem quiz	12
How to create your affirmation	16
Three vital love actions	19
How the law of attraction does not work	23
Attitude is everything	24
Romantic at heart quiz	27
How to tell the difference between personality and character traits	33
Health and well-being relationship quiz	36
Characteristics to avoid	41
Healthy characteristics	49
Testosterone: Man vs Woman	50
Faith and desire	53
Visualize	54
Gratitude	55
Love ingredient list	55
What to do with the love ingredient list	60
Ask your divine spirit	62

HOW THE LAW OF ATTRACTION WORKS

Attraction all begins with you. Everything we do or say, every movement we make sends out energy. This energy goes out to the universe and brings like energy back to us. If this energy is not specifically directed, it brings back to us lost tickets, lost sunglasses, money losses and the wrong guy! Yes even the wrong guy! It is important to give a specific purpose to the energy we send out because it is what we get back. Like attracts like which equals the law of attraction.

Our subconscious mind accepts what we believe and the universe supports our mind! We create our own experiences through our feelings and thoughts, without even knowing it. Whatever thought we entertain in our conscious mind goes directly into our subjective mind that accepts this thought as real without any judgment from our mind. This brings our desires, beliefs and thoughts no matter what they are into reality. Our mind accepts whatever we feed it without any judgment.

It is important to know and remember that it is the combination of your thoughts and feelings together that creates the law of attraction. Whatever you are feeling and thinking at any point in time is creating the law of attraction.

If you think and feel good that is the vibration that you send out to the universe and receive back. When you are negative and complain all the time the universe recognizes this too and sends it back to you. This same law also applies to attracting your man.

If you are tired of meeting Mr. Wrong and want to meet your ultimate man than you need to take some necessary actions provided in this guide to make this desire come about. Even by purchasing this guide you have already sent a message out to the Universe that you are seeking your ultimate man, the law of attraction is already at work!

Sharon manifested her ultimate man by using the law of attraction. Before Sharon applied the law of attraction she kept attracting men with the same characteristics, they were all workaholics. It was always a deep seeded desire that her man always had a steady job. The law of attraction always delivered her desires of a "man with a job". Sharon's desire came at a cost to her relationships though. Because Sharon's man never had time for vacations or family functions she had to go places and do things by herself. This ultimately did not work for Sharon as her man never had time for her or other functions as "he had a job to tend to". The universe always delivered her a man with a job.

Sharon had decided to leave her second marriage and underwent an emotional face to face experience with her inner self. She prepared a list and analyzed all the past relationships she had experienced. She could see her pattern in her actions in all of her relationships. Sharon was willing to grow so she embraced some of her fears instead of running from them. Sharon was able to get emotionally and spiritually in touch with herself, which resulted in her getting very clear about what she truly desired and what she was willing to do to get it.

Sharon created a *vision board* of the ultimate man of her dreams. The vision board included pictures such as flower and vegetable gardens, property in the country, camping, bike riding and vacation destinations. Sharon even added some old theatre tickets she kept from Phantom of the Opera. The theatre was something she quite enjoyed attending and wanted her man to also enjoy the theatre. Sharon was very passionate about finding the right man.

For forty days Sharon would light a candle and meditate upon her desires of her ultimate man. After the forty days she simply went about her daily life. Sharon had *faith* that she would meet her ultimate man and her faith was right! The universe delivered the opportunity for her to meet her ultimate man. When the universe first delivered this man to Sharon, she turned him down, not once but twice! Since the universe does not ever stop working, Sharon finally agreed to go out. Sharon knew in the first few dates she had finally found her ultimate man. Sharon's desires of her ultimate man came about by applying the law of attraction and the rest they say is history!

RELATIONSHIP REVIEW

It's always far easier to see the negative behaviors in a failed relationship. The negatives are key elements as to why you attracted the wrong guy in the first place. Take some time and examine what might be keeping your ultimate man away, it could be things such as old love beliefs or holding on to past relationship experiences. Do you see a pattern in the men you attract? Do you see a pattern in your choices? Do you or did you speak up in your relationships or did you sit quietly; did you do stupid things or say something that you later regretted? Did you get yelled at a lot or put down?

Has your love gone sour? Are you blaming yourself or others for your relationship issues? Are you emotionally drained after a break up? Are you being emotionally honest with yourself and others?

It is in your best interest to first face those hurtful experiences and then *release* those past experiences. Learn to forgive yourself and forgive others! Move forward with self- love, love for others, gratitude, faith and desire knowing that your man is out there and that the law of attraction will respond to your true desires!

RELATIONSHIP RED FLAGS

Below are some unhealthy relationship characteristics. Can you relate to any of these negative behaviors in your past relationships?

You are doing all the relationship work. If you found yourself doing all the fixing of what's wrong in your relationships and your partner refuses to participate this is not your man. Relationships are 100/100 not 100/0 not 50/50. Putting yourself last you will finish last. Your man should hold up his end of the relationship and not expect you to do all the changing or all the relationship work!

You do not feel important to your partner. Everyone in a relationship should feel important to one another. This is a vital need for all relationships to survive. Your man will not only tell you that you're important to him, he will show you how important you are to him.

You feel like you are walking on egg shells around your partner and avoid rocking the boat at certain times. You are not living in harmony and in fact it is a form of abuse when you are treated this way in a relationship. The universe is trying to tell you that this type of man is not your man! Your man should not make you feel like you are walking on eggshells and would not want you to feel this way.

You have been abused even in the slightest. Abuse in the slightest form is not a sign of a loving, healthy, caring relationship and should be treated as a serious problem with the abuser. You absolutely deserve to be in a loving relationship with no abuse in any way, shape or form. It is your right! Physical abuse is just not limited to physical force; locking you in a room or standing too close. Holding or hugging you when it is unwanted is also considered abuse. Restraining, shoving, shaking, choking, poking and pulling hair, hitting by using any weapon, objects or hands is abuse. Abuse can come in many forms such as withholding sex, refusing to have sex and a total lack of intimacy. These are all characteristics of sexual abuse. Hounding your partner for sex, forcing sex, being rough and treating you as a sex object is considered sexual abuse. Below are more forms of abuse.

- Using a person's spiritual beliefs to dominate, manipulate or control

- Slamming doors, throwing, breaking things, harming pets and throwing your clothes out and not letting you see your friends.

- Withholding money, making decisions on how the money is spent and using a credit card without permission is financial abuse.

Abuse is abuse when it is unwanted and/or unwelcomed behavior, be it; emotional, verbal, physical, social, sexual, financial, spiritual or psychological. Your ultimate man will not abuse you in any way, shape or form. PERIOD!

You are paying the way all the time. There is helping out and there is paying the way all the time. If you're paying the way all the time sorry to say but this is a mother-child relationship and it shows they have no real drive for success. When you have a grown man that is more than capable of working everyday but makes excuses why he can't work then you need not be supporting him fully. If you are paying the way now you will be paying the way in the future. Sure people lose their jobs, get injured or sick that's a little different. Everyone deserves a helping hand. You deserve your ultimate man to contribute positively in all ways to the relationship including financially.

You defend your partner. If you have defended your partner for his offensive behaviors and negative attitude that he always carries with him than you are not living in harmony with yourself. When you defend something or someone, you will bring things in your life that you do not want. Your man will not require any defending and will focus on solutions, not problems.

You are not being your ultimate self if you are hiding, ignoring or denying any of your emotional feelings. This is not part of self-love. If most of your relationships have failed, this is the time to do some inner work as to why you attract certain types of men. Get real with yourself first and foremost, so you can learn your patterns and stop attracting Mr. Wrong. If you are constantly attracting Mr. Wrong, you must analyze why. If you are accommodating whatever man that just happens to pass by then you are not being true to yourself, you are settling and settling will not bring you your ultimate match.

SELF ESTEEM QUIZ

How is your self-esteem these days? How are you really feeling about yourself? Sometimes we lose a little self-esteem without realizing it. You cannot feed your mind enough positive thoughts and feelings when it comes to self-esteem. Self-esteem plays a valuable role in our lives, it helps us understand who we are and in turn we are able to understand others. When your self-esteem is high, you are confident. If you have too low self-esteem you may find it hard to be in a healthy relationship. You might also beat yourself up and blame yourself for things that are not your fault. When we punish ourselves, we generally punish ourselves more harshly than others ever would. Each person may have different reasons for low self-esteem. You may have low self-esteem because you have never been taught how to have healthy self-esteem or what a healthy self-esteem even is. You learn to set new healthier boundaries when you have a high self-esteem which results in healthier relationships with everyone in your life.

Take a moment to think each question through. Simply choose yes or no to the following questions:

Do you deal with your short comings without casting blame?	Y	N
Are you open to constructive criticism and acknowledge your own mistakes?	Y	N
Are you comfortable giving and receiving compliments?	Y	N
Are you able to express your appreciation to others?	Y	N
Do you communicate clearly without being over bearing, angry or aggressive and without offending that person?	Y	N
Do you manage your feelings and emotions in a healthy manner?	Y	N
Does your inner harmony match your outer harmony? Meaning your saying and doing are in sync. Your expression is matching your action.	Y	N
Do you act with honesty, integrity and compassion?	Y	N
Do you love and appreciate yourself?	Y	N

Add up all your "yes" answers and see where your self-esteem sits.

7-9 yes answers
You have a healthy self-esteem.
You are being true to you and are being your ultimate self. The higher our inner feeling of ourselves enables us to cope with life's challenges. You are able to form healthy relationships. Self-esteem can make you resilient to trials and tribulations. The healthier your self-esteem the more likely you are to be ambitious and successful. You do not lose yourself to a relationship. Having authentic self-esteem means that you do not compare yourself to others and do not act in a competitive manner. You do not sit on the rotted dock waiting for your ship to come in, you swim to it!

4-6 yes answers
You have an average self-esteem.
If your score is average, there is something missing from your views or perhaps there is some uncertainty that you may have about your feelings. You may feel confident and happy in one area but not another. Look back through the questions and see where you can improve upon those missing yes answers. What are the missing things you can work on to set yourself into your healthy self-esteem? Are you being true to your feelings? Read more below on how affirmations can easily and effortlessly improve your enjoyment of life and what life has to offer

from the inside out with being your ultimate self.

Below 3 yes answers
You have depleted self-esteem.
The good news here is that there is something easy you can practice to re-inflate your self-esteem and be your ultimate self. Review the questions again and adapt some positive affirmations into your everyday routine. Self-esteem is for us to have and hold. Some just need help tapping into their *available* self-esteem. When you make positive affirmations part of your daily routine, you will feel and see the benefits first hand! Saying affirmations not only replaces your old programming, it strengthens you! You will be much more apt to say no without feeling guilty. You become more open to constructive criticism, acknowledge mistakes because you know that you are not perfect, you learn from them and grow. You will have a better balanced mind. You will not see trouble and failure when you have a healthy self-esteem. Get to know yourself, fill yourself up with love and accept your own uniqueness. This is your birthright!

HOW TO CREATE YOUR AFFIRMATION

Affirmations are a positive way to convey our likes, desires and goals out to the universe. Affirmations are power of suggestion. Affirmation in the dictionary states its meaning; to declare positively and be willing to stand by the truth. If you want to attract the ultimate man then affirmations will play a key role! Applying the power of suggestion through an affirmation is part of the law of attraction. An affirmation re-enforces your specific desire, belief and faith to the universe. To enforce the law of attraction, you will want to create your own affirmation for manifesting your ultimate man! To get the most benefit from your affirmation is to say it in present tense. Say the affirmation as though it is already happening.

As we live in an electronic world, we still need to occasionally get out that pencil and paper and state our desires in writing. By writing your affirmation out you shift your mind focus and your desires to come about.

By stating an affirmation with I am or I have, you are giving that affirmation greater power. Affirmations can be used for any of your desires such as increasing your income, change a career or perhaps you want to lose some weight. Apply affirmations to help you work through the tribulations at work. Affirmations can simply just raise your spirits if you say them with meaning from your soul.

Start with the affirmation below as part of your daily routine or you can adapt the affirmations and create your own. The important thing to remember is to get in the practice of saying affirmations every day and say them with conviction!

"I give myself permission to release and let go of all negative self-limiting thoughts that I grew up with. I am now choosing a healthy self-esteem for my highest good. By eliminating my self-negative talk and excuses, I am now able to love my mind, body, spirit and soul and see its beauty that lingers in myself every day. Each new day, I create a whole bunch of new loving thoughts about myself that brings me an abundance of confidence and self-love. I am deserving of true love, joy and happiness."

One way to get in the habit of saying affirmations is every time you wash your hands in the washroom, look in the mirror and try this affirmation jingle.

"I love, cherish and approve of myself today and every day in each and every loving way" or "I am feeling great about myself today and every day in every loving way and nobody can take that away."

Below are some other affirmations you can adapt to your everyday routine.

> ***"I am unique and I am me; I love being me."***

> ***"I am beautiful and everyone loves me."***

> ***"I am manifesting love and I am truly loved."***

Affirmations said aloud open your subconscious mind! The more you affirm your mind, the more your mind accepts it as real and turns your desires into your reality. You can also simply record your affirmation(s) on a recording device to play first thing in the morning when you wake up and then again before you go to bed. Ensure that it is *you* recording *your* affirmation. Listen as many times as you wish to your affirmation.

THREE VITAL LOVE ACTIONS TO RELATIONSHIPS

You should feel *loved, important* and *appreciated* by your man; however you should feel these things first and foremost about yourself, regardless of any man in your life. Love yourself first, if you don't, no one else really will either. You are the most important person to you! Without you, you cannot be important to anyone else. Always appreciate yourself first through your own gratitude. When you appreciate yourself first with the amazing things you can do or natural born gifts you were afforded, you will also be appreciated by others. Giving and receiving love, feeling and being important and appreciated are the three basic needs for love and a continuation of love. We all need to give love and all of us need to give love back, but we have to give it first to get it back. It is vital to our relationships to be and feel important, appreciated and loved for both people in the relationship. Affairs can happen because one or more of these three love actions were not being met.

Accept love and give love. Forgive and make peace with your past. Keep the lesson and throw away the experience. Finding faults, complaining and nagging is not giving love. Spread love to others through kindness, encouragement and gratitude. It's that simple. Love is a gift, use it, it is the cheapest, easiest and best thing you can do for yourself and others. There is no stronger power in your mind than the power of love. Without love you cannot attract love so let go of past experiences.

Lucy could attract the most handsome men but those handsome men all had the same thing in common! None of them were emotionally available. Because Lucy was the loving caregiver, people pleasing and takes care of her man type; she always attracted men who needed a care giving type of woman. Lucy did some break downs of her and Mr. Wrong's behaviors in past relationships. She was able to see the pattern of her attracting Mr. Wrong and also uncovered that she lived many years through old love beliefs, instead of her *own* beliefs. Lucy had not been honest and truthful about how she felt about her own feelings in any relationship she encountered. She would give her heart away to make someone else happy and lost herself in every relationship. Lucy never ever felt appreciated by her man. Lucy often discounted her own feelings and put others ahead. By analyzing each past relationship Lucy uncovered that each relationship was missing at least *one* of the three *vital* love actions! No wonder the relationships never worked out.

On a blank sheet of paper write out each name of a significant relationship down the left hand side like the sample provided below.

NAME	DID I FEEL LOVED?	DID I FEEL IMPORTANT?	DID I FEEL APPRECIATED?
BERT	YES	NO	NO
BOB	YES	NO	NO
DANNY	NO	NO	NO

The above list gives you an example to get going on your own list. There is no right or wrong to the list. The point is to see if there is a repeat pattern in *who* you are attracted to and how you *felt* in each relationship.

Your list could be ten pages long, that's okay. The main goal is to uncover *who* you are attracting and *why*. Lucy was easily able to identify some vital love actions were missing because she was not giving herself one hundred percent love, appreciation and importance first and therefore she uncovered that she "attracted" the same type of characteristics in her relationships.

LOVE IS…..

- **Being honest with your feelings**
- **Giving/Receiving**
- **Patient and kind**
- **Forgiving**
- **Understanding**

LOVE IS NOT….

- *Being dishonest with your feelings*
- *People pleasing*
- *A possession*
- *Controlling*
- *Ignoring/blaming*

HOW THE LAW OF ATTRACTION DOES NOT WORK

There is one important point/rule that you must know about using the law of attraction. It cannot be willed upon another person that you already truly desire, it does not work that way.

For example, the law does not work to attract a particular person that already exists that you are madly in love with and this person shows no interest in you. If you think of it this way, what if someone was madly in love with you but you did not feel the same way about that person; would you want them to be able to will you to be with them? Of course not! Sometimes we are convinced that someone is right for us when the truth is, they are not in harmony with you and the universe can see that but we can't so we sometimes relentlessly try over and over only to discover in the end, it was not meant to be. As we grow and evolve; our frequency and inner harmony can change. When that change occurs it is because that person is not your ultimate match for life, perhaps someone else is to be your ultimate man. Bigger and better than the one who broke your heart. The law of attraction can bring people together as well as move people apart. The law lives in you, in everyone.

ATTITUDE IS EVERYTHING

Many women also feel they can change their man in some form so that eventually he will see how really great you are and fall madly in love with you. It does not work that way, in actuality you push people away when you try to change who they are, because you are not truly accepting them for who they are. You're accepting them with the hopes of changing them. You cannot change anyone and it is truly a waste of time. You're sending a message that they are not good enough as they are now. We can certainly do our best to influence people but we cannot change people. This is not acting in a loving way. If you always feel a need to change the man than you are with than he is not the ultimate man for you!

If you have the attitude of "all the good guys are gone" or "I will never meet anyone" deep down what you are really trying to say is "I wish I had a healthy stable relationship". Thinking reverse psychology will not bring you what you want, it actually sends mixed signals to the universe. The universe is not sure exactly what you are asking for so you get nothing in return. The law of attraction is always at work even when it doesn't work, it *is* working. If you are always negatively stating "I'll never meet anyone", well you're right; you won't because you keep telling the universe that so the universe responds with nothing. Be careful of how and what you are asking the universe for. The universe always responds everyday of your life. So now when someone asks you, "how is the dating going?" instead of responding with I keep meeting the wrong guy, reply with "I will meet my ultimate man when the time is right." That is a positive re-enforcement that sends that message out to the universe. It takes time to reprogram your negative thoughts. But as you become more aware of the negative you will correct it with a positive thought! Positive thoughts are food for your brain. If you keep saying I keep meeting the wrong guy, you will keep meeting the wrong guy. What you put out to the universe you get back. Ensure you practice positive thoughts and statements in your everyday life.

Don't be concerned about who, what, where and when you are going to meet your man. Let the universe take care of that. The universe will deliver the ultimate man. Do not waste your time on someone who does not, cannot or will not love you back in harmony. Be true to you. Be true to yourself and get ready to meet your ultimate man!

An affirmation for manifesting your ultimate man might sound like one of these:

"I am easily attracting my ultimate man for me, my soul mate, and my partner for life."

"I am attracting my soul mate, for which we share an unbreakable bond. We are together at the perfect time in a healthy and positive way."

"Love opens all doors and I am attracting my ultimate soul mate."

"Divine love is in control and I will meet my ultimate man at the perfect time."

"Divine love foresees everything and provides my ultimate man now. My divine love now appears."

You can create your own affirmations to suit you best. Create your affirmation to be in the present tense like you already "have" your ultimate man.

TAKE THIS QUIZ TO FIND OUT IF YOU ARE A ROMANTIC AT HEART

What is your idea of being romantic?

1. You see fairy tales as….
a) So romantic, I fall hook, line and sinker!
b) Just a fairy tail.
c) Boring.

2. Romance to you is….
a) Your man bringing you home a sweet favourite treat after a stressful workday.
b) Cheesy.
c.) Pure Bliss.

3. What best describes your perfect afternoon date with your man?
a) Lunch at a coffee shop.
b) Picnic in the park.
c) Not sure, we just usually hang out.

4. Your man texted you and is going to give you a nice back massage tonight, you feel:

a) So excited that you are going to treat him tomorrow to something real sweet.

b) Have a good chuckle and think yeah right that's not going happen.

c) Daydream of coming home to candles and massage oils.

5. Your best friend tells you she met her perfect hunk. You think to yourself:
a) Awesome I hope it all works out.
b) I can hardly wait to meet my ultimate man like that.
c) Be careful there girl friend.

6. Its Valentine's Day and you are in a relationship, what are your expectations from your man?

a) Hope to get a little something.

b) A dinner out or do something special. This is his time to show how much he cares.

c) Nothing really, Valentine's Day is just another day.

7. Right in the middle of amazing sex, the man you have been dating for one month tells you he has feelings for you for the very first time; you think to yourself…..
a) Are you kidding me, right in the middle of sex!
b) Yes, we are taking our relationship to the next level.
c) Wow, he is really opening up to me.

8. If your man forgets your anniversary, you:
a) Shrug it off as no big deal.
b) Be a little hurt but give a second chance for him to make it up.
c) Upset, hurt and a little bit angry! It is clear he is not too concerned about the relationship.

9. How much time do you expect to spend with a man that you are becoming serious with?
a) Every single day.
b) Three to four days per week.
c) Doesn't matter.

10. What best describes the endings of your previous relationships?
a) He felt you were not into the relationship.
b) Mutual split, we both knew it was not meant to be.
c) He felt smothered and could not be that guy for me.

Match up your answers with the scale below. Total all your points together for your score.

SCORING

QUESTIONS	A	B	C
1	2	1	0
2	1	0	2
3	1	2	0
4	1	0	2
5	1	2	0
6	1	2	0
7	0	2	1
8	0	1	2
9	2	1	0
10	0	1	2
Total			

If you scored **fifteen** points or more:

Hopeless Romantic

You are a hopelessly devoted romantic at heart, but your romantic expectations could be getting in your own way of a happy and satisfying relationship. Chances are if you are always looking for that one who will sweep you off of your feet; you will always be disappointed as you are putting fairy tale expectations out to the universe. Your Prince Charming is out there but he may not come with the fairy tale ending that you expect. Take answers from this quiz to analyze your real expectations versus your fantasies of your knight in shining armor.

If you scored **seven** to **fourteen** points:
Romantic at heart

You view romance a two way street. As you are a confident woman you do not expect to be constantly showered with romance as you choose to find that silver lining in your man if he misses an occasion. You also will not wait around for romance; you find other ways to keep your romance alive! You go girl!

If you scored **six** or **fewer** points: ## *Resistant Romantic*

You are a no TLC for me kind of woman. This can be true in women who have been hurt, betrayed or rejected in the past. Let go of those old past hurts and give yourself permission to be romanced again! If you constantly send out vibes to the universe that you dislike or do not need any romance in your life than that is what you get back. Put a little romance in your heart and watch your relationship sizzle!

"Romantic fantasies can lessen pain and promote relaxation. Your anxiety levels will also drop whether your thoughts are that of real or imagined romantic fantasy. Go ahead and fantasize, its healthy for you."

HOW TO TELL THE DIFFERENCE BETWEEN PERSONALITY AND CHARACTER TRAITS

It is very important that you do not confuse personalities with characteristics. These two really differ from one another. The personality of someone is usually fairly easy to read such as funny, shy or energetic, these are personalities. We tend to connect with personality traits rather than character. Personality presents itself on the outside, not the inside. It takes longer to learn someone's character than it does their personality. Your character reflects your morals such as honesty, respect, trust, leadership, courage etc. They can be talkative and affectionate with a great sense of humor! Knowing the difference between characteristics and personality can save your heart and your wallet! Yes your wallet! Con artists, narcissists and players all have great personalities but some really lack in great character! Lots of people have a great personality but lack in the character department. Knowing the difference is important! Knowing what to look for will save you heartache. You cannot tell a person's character by merely talking to them on the phone once or by texting all day and night. To see a person's true character takes some time and you should take some time to get to know and see their character in them by physical interaction.

It could be as simple as meeting for coffee or a walk in the country side or by a lake. You can learn a lot about someone's character when you see them interact with others, not just how they interact with you.

A person with good character expresses their inner self, their morals and integrity. They can show compassion and understanding. They are able to enjoy being in a romantic healthy relationship. A person with great character tends to protect their health, well-being and self-esteem despite problems or any chaos. They possess a positive can do attitude and accept people for who they are. They have the ability to influence others. They act courageous, always alert and are seeking to learn new things and find solutions. They do not feel scared to get to a personal level with people. A person with great character also does not play games. They do not make you guess at what or how they feel. They will tell you how they feel and their actions match the words they speak.

Once you learn to recognize the characteristics of the player, the con artist and the narcissist, you will be able to differentiate quickly between the men who are just trying to get laid and the men that display a healthy character about them. Knowing what to look for and knowing what you truly desire, need and want in your ultimate man will eliminate so much wasted time with Mr. Wrong.

HEALTH AND WELL BEING RELATIONSHIP QUIZ

Do you experience healthy relationships or are you accepting unhealthy abusive relationships? Take this quiz to find out if you experience healthy or unhealthy relationships. Answer each question based on your previous relationship experiences. If you are in a relationship, answer each question based on how you are currently treated.

Simply answer each question below with a Yes or No answer.

		Y	N	PTS
1.	My man gives me my own space	Y	N	PTS
2.	My man is supportive of my hobbies and activities I enjoy doing	Y	N	PTS
3.	My man supports and encourages me to pursue new things that I want to try	Y	N	PTS
4.	My man makes and takes time to listen and talk with me	Y	N	PTS
5.	My man thinks I spend too much time fussing on my appearance when going out	Y	N	PTS

6. My man must remain in constant contact with me	Y	N	PTS
7. My family and friends do not care for my man	Y	N	PTS
8. My man displays jealous and possessive behaviors	Y	N	PTS
9. My man claims that I am too much into other activities	Y	N	PTS
10. My man likes to control what I wear and how I look	Y	N	PTS
11. I have been called a flirter and a cheat	Y	N	PTS
12. I must always check in with my man because he wants me to	Y	N	PTS
13. My man often embarrasses me in front of others	Y	N	PTS
14. My man often tells me what I should be doing and who I should and should not associate with	Y	N	PTS
15. I am often kept isolated from my family and friends	Y	N	PTS
16. I walk on egg shells and feel uneasy	Y	N	PTS
17. My man most times places blame and fault on	Y	N	PTS

~ CJ Moore's Bachelorette Classified Dating Guide ~

everyone but himself			
18. My man displays passive/aggressive behaviors	Y	N	PTS
19. Threatens to destroy my belongings, my family and your friends	Y	N	PTS
20. Criticizes and calls me names	Y	N	PTS
21. My man is manipulative through destructive behaviors	Y	N	PTS
22. Has threatened to commit suicide	Y	N	PTS
23. Pressures and or tries to manipulate sexual encounters	Y	N	PTS
24. Puts me down by saying degrading and hurtful things	Y	N	PTS
25. Threatens to physically harm me and my belongings	Y	N	PTS
26. Has physically abused me in anyway	Y	N	PTS
TOTAL	Y	N	PTS

Questions one to four
Give yourself *one* point for every NO answer
Total____

Questions five to eight
Give yourself *one* point for every YES answer
Total____

Scoring: Questions nine to twenty-six
Give yourself *five* points for every YES answer
Total____

Add total points together and see which health category you belong to.

ZERO POINTS-Healthy

Finally a zero score is great! You not only maintain a healthy relationship but you have the ability to recognize unhealthy behaviors. You keep the communication lines open!

ONE TO TWO POINTS-Semi Healthy

Ensure you keep the communication lines open at all times! It is very important that you speak your truth of your likes and dislikes with your man! Watch for any old or new behavioral patterns that may develop. Communication is crucial when it comes to building healthy relationships.

THREE TO FOUR POINTS- Unhealthy/Mistreated

If you experience any form of abusive behavior, this is not a healthy relationship. Abuse in any form is very toxic and can lead to destruction of your life!

FIVE TO TEN POINTS- Abused/Harmed

If you have scored five points chances are you have been in an abusive relationship in some form. These types of experiences can strip you of self-esteem piece by piece. That is what abusers do. They will try to break you by saying hurtful and threatening things. Review your answers to uncover your past experience so you know what to watch for when it comes to abusive situations.

ELEVEN POINTS PLUS-Abused

You have definitely been in an abusive relationship. It is your birthright to live without any abuse in your life. Recognizing signs of abuse can save your life and allow you to live your ultimate life; being your ultimate self without any form of abuse. Refer to the relationship red flag section for information on abuse and all different forms of abuse. You deserve a loving and caring relationship.

CHARACTERISTICS TO AVOID

The Player Characteristics

The player feels comfortable with you, with himself and with others. The player's intention is not to get seriously involved in a relationship. Some players may casually date while others are just out for one night of fun and sex.

Here are some tell-tale signs of the Player.

- The player is only available on his terms. You may casually date for months but it never goes to the next level. If you dare ask for a commitment, he may break off with you or have the attitude of let's just keep going with the flow and see where it leads.

- The player will probably not want to meet your family and really does not want you to meet his family either. If you do happen to meet his family, contact will be limited. Generally players do not commit to any one person. A player may, however, have a few ladies on the go at one time.

- The Player will have very limited contact with you. Contact could be limited to text or computer contact. The player keeps many friends and generally does not give out much information even when asked. Nothing stands between his friends and his hobbies or sports, not even you.

- The player will flirt with you and compliment you. The player is well skilled in the bedroom and he should be as he has a lot of experience. If you are rushed into sex or if he seems rushed or crushed for time then chances are you met the player.

- The player is not emotionally available for you. Be wary of newly single men fresh out of long term relationships.

The player is generally not shy. You will always tell a player as they want sex the first time they lay eyes on you, they are really not interested in deep conversation about life. The player may or may not be in a relationship with someone else, some men will openly admit they are happily married and just seeking a one night stand while others hide it from you.

The player is not a bad person. In fact, players can be really great guys and they too are looking for that one girl that makes their heart flutter and sing but in the meantime they play the field. If you are not part of their game, you won't get hurt.

The Con Artist Characteristics

The con artist is so sleek that you did not see him coming. The con artist is the nicest manipulating, generous and easy going person you would want to meet. They practically sweep you off your feet. Con artists prey on independent and dependent women. They do not always have a preference, just a motive!

- Con artists appear very cool and calm. They have a love for life. Because the con artist does not want you to figure them out they will go to great lengths to hide information about themselves. They like to talk and boast about people they supposedly know that have some sort of authority.

- The con artist may talk of his tied up money or perhaps he is expecting an investment or inheritance one day. The con artist paints a very pretty picture of himself. They do this to appear that they have so much to offer one day when the money is not tied up.

- Some con artists have a laziness about them. They do not want to work at anything; that is why they con you. It's easier for them to manipulate you than get off their butts and physically do something. Con artists will often disengage from too much work.

- Con artists will not likely introduce you to his family. If they do, contact will be extremely limited. A con artist does not want to be discovered by their own family.

- Another sign of the con artist is he has no job or is in-between jobs. Con artists also move quite frequently, they do not always remain idle in one place for very long. They easily move onto the next victim.

- Con artists easily forget their wallets and will have no problem asking to borrow cash from you. They are master manipulators they make up the most believable stories as to why they need to borrow money. In the very beginning con artists do pay you back because they want you to trust them. Some may even offer to leave you something of value until they repay you. In the end if you are not careful they will take your money and run.

Obviously con artists have the capabilities to con; through lying, cheating and stealing even from their own parents and children. Con artists play and prey on your emotions. They have no conscience so they can easily manipulate you. Con artists go through life obtaining what they want by manipulating people. If a con artist can land a sugar mama he is in heaven! He will eat, drink and party, all on your dime. Don't give him the dime!

The Narcissist Characteristics

Narcissism is a personality disorder that differs from narcissistic tendencies. Someone can have narcissistic tendencies yet still have the ability to show empathy and compassion for others. The same trait that these two share is that they are the victim in any circumstance. They cast blame upon others. A narcissist is excessively self-absorbed in their personal comfort. They have a self-love unlike a selfish person.

Here are the tell-tale signs of a person with narcissism:

- Nothing is their fault! They feel victim to all situations in their life and are very quick to cast blame. They have the attitude that they have done nothing wrong. They will right their every wrong whether it's through blame or playing a victim role. You might hear a narcissist often say I did nothing wrong.

- When you meet a narcissist you will also meet someone who is charming and loves to have fun. They can be very generous, are not bad people and love in their own way; however, narcissists are not emotionally available. They do not have the ability to feel or show empathy. Narcissists can hug you and say they care but they cannot back that up, they are not capable of a healthy love and affection on a "consistent" basis.

- Takes no ownership to any failed relationships. These relationships include ex partners, parents, siblings, grandparents, friends you name it. Narcissists are not very forgiving. If a narcissist is unhappy with you, he can erase you out of his life no matter who you are. Narcissists will claim they did everything possible to make their relationships work. They always argue it was their partner's entire fault. A narcissist will cheat and turn around and place blame on their partner, they will give any excuse that fits their victim behavior. The point here is that they place blame upon others and never take any responsibility for any failed relationships.

- Narcissists often speak so much of their ex partners good and bad habits that you will feel like you actually know their ex! You will notice that the narcissist will only ever speak of his version of the events that took place in the past. They want you to perceive them as king of his castle and if he has a bad habit well you know why, it's his exes fault and that makes his fault ok.

- Controlling and manipulative behavior is often displayed by the narcissist. Narcissists like to control their relationships with people. They even control the lack of a relationship using manipulation. They can use manipulation in form of gifts or mementos of theirs that they give to you because you are so special. In the end though when all is said and done and whether they or you have ended the relationship, even if you mutually agree to end the relationship, guess what? They are the victim and they cast blame on you.

- Another form of controlling behavior of a narcissist is they can also withhold things from you such as items of clothing, money, sex and talking! They can go for long periods without talking to you and it's your fault that they are not talking to you. You cannot win. Sometimes they will give you something and when they get angry and upset with you, they just freely take it back. Narcissists, if he is of the jealous type, can alienate you from your friends. Narcissists are also not always freely available.

- Narcissists will see the bad side of the coin before the good side in most cases. They can have a negative attitude on one thing and a positive attitude on another. Most times it just depends what mood they are in! Narcissists are generally moody characters. Sometimes they can just go into hiding for a few days from the world. They at times can make you feel like a million dollars and the next day ignore you.

- Narcissists can often feel anger and even rage over pretty much anything that has hurt their feelings. They can be very boisterous and yell and say hurtful things and blame you or others for their state of mind. Narcissists can also be quiet and private and enter into depressed states of mind because they are so angry. They cannot acknowledge nor see how they can be any part of their state of mind. Whether angry, mad or sad narcissists blame their state of mind on others.

- It is a vicious blame game with a narcissist. If you make a suggestion or solution to their problem they will find an excuse or another fault in your suggestion. They will excuse and validate their behaviors by playing the victim role.

Narcissists often have a great skill or ability of some sort and are generally helpful and very knowledgeable people. Narcissists make for good friends and come in all shapes and sizes, male or female. It takes a very special kind of person to love another with narcissism disorder.

Some people can have a few "narcissistic" traits but not be a person with "narcissism disorder". Narcissism is a disorder that can be treated however, only in long term therapy after the person can admit they have a disorder. Those ones with the disorder feel that they do not have any problems, it is everyone else's fault and are very reluctant to seek professional help or advice for this disorder.

HEALTHY CHARACTERISTICS TO LOOK FOR

People with healthy characteristics have a strong faith in themselves and are achievers of happiness as they are honest with their feelings and emotions. A person who has uniqueness to them is that of a healthy character because they are content with whom they are in their mind because they accept themselves completely. A person with a healthy character also has the ability to recognize their flaws and not so great habits; and they are always striving to learn new things. People with healthy characteristics are also confident without the self-glorifying attitude. You will see below the three love actions that are part of a healthy character. Can you see yourself and your ultimate man in here anywhere?

- Protect their well-being despite any type of roadblocks such as trials and tribulations.

- Respectful to their self and others.

- Confident with a healthy level of self-esteem.

- Have goals and plans for the future.

- Ability to demonstrate feelings of *appreciation*

- Do not want to change people, they accept people as they are.

- Able to be in a *loving* romantic relationship. Shows compassion.

- Ability to communicate with anyone. Understanding to others and their *importance*.

- Live with great conviction. They listen with their mind and display a positive body language.

- Display competent behavior and put their courage to good use.

TESTOSTERONE: *MAN VS WOMAN*

A healthy level of testosterone plays a key role in a man's wellbeing. Having too low of testosterone can play havoc on a man. Too low of testosterone levels can cause men to lose interest in sex (pull back), erectile dysfunction and feelings of depression. It can also affect his level of concentration. As men age their testosterone levels also naturally decline. When a man falls in love, he loses testosterone, while women on the other hand experience an increase of testosterone when they fall in love.

A man with higher levels of testosterone may have strong physical features such as a large adams apple, broad shoulders, strong jaw line and facial hair. Women are generally attracted to men who have higher levels of testosterone. Studies have also shown that when a man has sex with new or multiple partners his testosterone levels are much higher. When sexually aroused testosterone levels are elevated in both men and women. Women who have higher levels of testosterone are more sexually active and more apt to achieve orgasm. Oxytocin is a "bonding hormone" that both men and women also have in common.

Testosterone however is known to suppress a man's oxytocin level. No wonder women can fall in love so easily!

FAITH AND DESIRE

Another part of the law of attraction is having faith and desire. With very strong faith and desire; the universe will respond by providing your ultimate man at the perfect time! You must have faith and belief that you are to meet your man at the perfect time. Do you have faith in yourself? When you believe in faith, you can overcome obstacles, trials and tribulations. If you feel like you have lost faith then apply more faith. It's that simple. When faith has failed you simply give yourself permission to have more faith than you ever had before.

To have a desire means to have a strong wish or craving. When you mix faith and desire you are in perfect harmony and when you are in perfect harmony the universe responds with your desire.

VISUALIZE

Visualize or picture your ultimate man in your mind daily. Concentrate on *feelings* of being with your ultimate man not his physical attributes and features. Feel yourself out doing something that you love doing with your man. Maybe you love the theatre, close your eyes and *feel* yourself being at the theatre with your man. Whatever it is that you desire, be it a bike ride you enjoy with your man or fishing. Just *feel* yourself doing things with your man. When you can consciously feel that you are already in possession of your desire it acts as a magnet. Consciously feeling your desire attracts your desire to you. You can also create a vision board to represent your desires. No matter what that desire is; be it a man, a trip, a boat, a painting, you get the picture! Take that desire and put it on a board that you see every day. Visualizing plays a key role in the law of attraction.

GRATITUDE

Another very significant part of the law of attraction is gratitude. It's important to be thankful for what we have no matter how big or small. Writing in a gratitude journal *everyday* can improve your immune system; give you a better night's sleep, just to name a few benefits. It provides you with a higher level of positive emotions so you're able to feel more joy and pleasure. Having gratitude also increases your self-esteem. Gratitude helps you stay focused to keep working toward your goals you wish to attain. Get in the habit every day of writing out the things in life that you are grateful for.

LOVE INGREDIENT LIST

If life was perfect and if you were to wake up tomorrow morning to your ultimate man, what would he be like? Take some time to really envision your ultimate man. How does your ultimate man make you feel? Is he affectionate, respectful, funny and hard working? What quality does he have that you love? What are your expectations of your ultimate Man? Too high of expectations can affect your relationships with anyone, especially your partner. Ensure your expectations are reachable and that you express your expectations in a healthy way. Do not be afraid to talk about what you expect, it could make or break your relationship if this is talked about up front. Your expectations should be clear and not set beyond something that is not reachable. For example if you expect your ultimate man to fix your car himself and he is not the least bit mechanically inclined, you are in for trouble, not only mechanically but you will continually be disappointed in an unrealistic expectation.

What character traits are important to you? In order to attract what we truly and deeply want, we must be very clear to the universe what type of man we really want in our lives. You must be very specific when creating your love ingredient list; a love ingredient list is the same as manifestation list, however, like a recipe, if you leave out a main ingredient or two and the results could be a disaster! Your love ingredients are essential and vital to your self-discovery and are necessary to attract your ultimate man. These are all very important steps in manifesting. Do not leave anything out or anything to chance. Take some time to really visualize yourself doing things with your man to help you with discovering your love ingredients that are essential to your inner soul and spirit.

Under each category write your own love ingredients. State only what you *do want*, not what you don't want. If any category is not important to you then skip it. The universe needs to hear specific positive information. Simply take what you do not want and re state it in what you do want! Remember to let the universe take care of what your man's "physical" attributes are to be.

Communication:
How do you want to communicate with your man, yell at each other all the time or discuss things as adults openly and calmly? Do you want your man to be emotionally available for you? Do you want your man to be able to come and talk to you?

_____

_____

Financial/Professional:
Is financial and/or professional status important to you? Do you desire that your man have millions of dollars? Remember to always be very specific. Mere wishing for a man for his money could bring disastrous results to your recipe! Get creative in inputting your love ingredients. Does your man work every day or part time? The important thing to remember is how your man going to *contribute* to the relationship. It doesn't have to be financially, there are many stay at home Dads out there.

Sometimes part time work brings in a full time pay!

___

___

Sexual appetite:
Go ahead and dare to write out your wildest love ingredients ever! Sex is an important function in maintaining a healthy relationship. Allowing joy and pleasure into the bedroom brings true essence to the relationship.

___

___

Spiritual:
What are your spiritual practices? Do you attend church every Sunday? Do you celebrate birthdays and special occasions? What are your moral values? These are all important love ingredients! It may not matter to you his spiritual side.

___

___

Compatibility:
Do you have a particular hobby that you hope to have in common your man? Does your man need to have a pretty good sense of humour? Take some time and think about compatibilities.

~ CJ Moore's Bachelorette Classified Dating Guide ~

You obviously want a man that is going to compliment your relationship. Does your man have to like dogs, cats, rats or snakes?

_____

_____

Other important love ingredients like family and family planning should be on your ingredient list if it is important to you. Whatever your desires write them out in your ingredient love list. If it's something that is not important to you, leave it out. You must be absolutely sure what characteristics and traits you want in your man. Whether you want your man to be able to build things with his hands or do all the cooking.

Whatever you're true desire is, list it on your love ingredients list. Always ensure it's a present list of ingredients.

Manifesting your ultimate man may not happen overnight! It may take several days, weeks or even months.

WHAT TO DO WITH THE LOVE INGREDIENT LIST

From the ingredient list you will be able to do two things, create your affirmation to say daily and manifest your ultimate man. The universe is always listening to your voice and your thoughts at all times so be sure to be specific and positive. Add this affirmation to your daily routine.

"I am worthy of love and love is worthy of me. I am now creating a very loving and lasting relationship. We are best friends and love fills our hearts desires. I am safe in love and we take care of each other. I bring out the best in him and he brings out the best in me."

When saying your affirmation, give it power by envisioning what you will be doing with your man. Perhaps you love sailing. Get on the boat with your ultimate man and let your mind set sail! Prefer to golf then same thing get out on the green and play your game with your ultimate man! Envision your thoughts to attract your heart's desire. You can also try this method. Most women like to slow dance. Put on a slow song, not a sappy song you are going to cry to but one that is inspiring to you. Get up and dance with yourself! Yes dance with yourself; this adds feeling and sends a powerful message to the universe. Think of the love ingredient list you created and feel yourself in the moment with your ultimate man; envision in your mind "that" you are with him already and you are ending the night with a meaningful slow dance.

ASK YOUR DIVINE SPIRIT

Being spiritually awakened, your feelings shift into neutral which is good because being neutral allows you to see that if you fuel an emotion or feeling with more attention than we are telling ourselves how to feel instead of asking our inner spirit to guide us into neutral. When you are in neutral, you are able to stay in touch with your inner self where no right or wrong exists, no victims, only peace and love. Your mind gets a break from negativity! It is re-fuelling to re-think. When the inner spirit of truth enters our mind, we have then entered into the soul of the real because we have taken full possession of our life and our destiny.

You may ask your divine spirit for guidance when you are unclear about something in your heart of hearts. Some may refer to this as a prayer or meditation. Perhaps you are frustrated or confused about something and you are unsure what to do. You can pray, meditate or call upon your divine spirit, at anytime, any day and anywhere!

Step One

Get comfortable. Take a few minutes and relax. Simply breathe in through your nose and release your breath out of your mouth slowly in the same rhythm for three to five minutes. This connects your mind and body and helps you stay focused. If you are A.D.D. you can ask that your mind please be still.

Call upon your divine spirit. You can do this by saying your own prayer or simply ask divine spirit to be of guidance.

Step Two

Ask your question to your divine spirit.

When asking your divine spirit for an answer to a question, you must ask only one specific question at a time. The answer for some people may come right away so keep a pen handy when asking. For others it may take hours to several days for the answer to come about. The answers may come in various forms. Do *not look* for the answers immediately, continue about your day and your life and listen carefully and be receptive to things as they happen. The answer will come. Someone may suddenly come into your life that provides you with the answer to question or you may happen to cross paths with a stranger that may hold the answer for you. It can come in form of a song that has a meaning. After a length of time has passed and you are still not getting an answer, you may ask your divine intuition for guidance and knowledge for the answer. Ask that the answer be very clear that you cannot mistake it. Apply this affirmation to not only man challenges but any challenges you may face *"divine intuition is now showing me the way by working in and working through me, revealing to me the perfect truth about this situation"*. It is important to be open and receptive to the answer. The answer may not be what you want to hear but you asked your divine spirit so understand that whatever the answer is, it's the universe doing this for your highest good.

If the law does not appear to be working for bringing about your man then get creative. If you sleep in the middle of your bed, try sleeping on one side only. Being an active participant plays a key role. Maybe you are not being specific enough or perhaps too specific on who, what, where and when's. Are you sitting and waiting passively for something to happen? Make some room in your closet for your man's belongings! The universe mirrors your thoughts and when you have constant negative thoughts the universe delivers negative things. Doubtful and negative thinking is not using or applying the law of attraction. Do not be afraid to feel like you already have your ultimate man. Feeling and seeing in your mind brings about your desires faster.

Are you serious about meeting your ultimate man or are you still mourning the loss of the last guy that took advantage of you or cheated on you? Are you still attached to conditioned beliefs? Have you fully explored your past relationships? Have you forgiven where forgiveness is needed? In order to move on you must release whatever it is that is holding you back. There are lots of singles programs out there. Join a social group through your local community organizations. Try volunteering for a few hours through a local volunteer organization. You just never know how the universe will bring about your man or what he will look like.

Practice self-love and self-growth using positive affirmations. Add a releasing affirmation if you are still stuck on Mr. Wrong. Simply reaffirm yourself, "I am willing to release and let go of what no longer serves me. I am at peace by letting go and moving forward." Add to your daily routine. Affirmations work best if they are changed up every forty to sixty days.

Women are not always true to themselves and often fear that if they desire something that it means they are too selfish or not deserving of it. You are actually not being your ultimate self if you are not in touch with your deserving desires. You absolutely deserve an abundance of love and happiness! You owe it to yourself to be your ultimate self to live in joy and harmony. Trust your desires no matter what they are or how crazy they may be, connect with them, do not be afraid, and be true to you.

"You can give love, show love, be love, but you cannot teach someone to love. It comes from within."

CJ Moore

About the author

CJ Moore is an insightful certified coach practitioner that specializes in personal growth and relationships. CJ knows firsthand how the law of attraction does and does not work.

To learn more about CJ and her dating principles, check out her blog at <u>cjmooresbacheloretteclassifieddatingguide @ wordpress.com</u>.

Made in the USA
Charleston, SC
31 May 2014